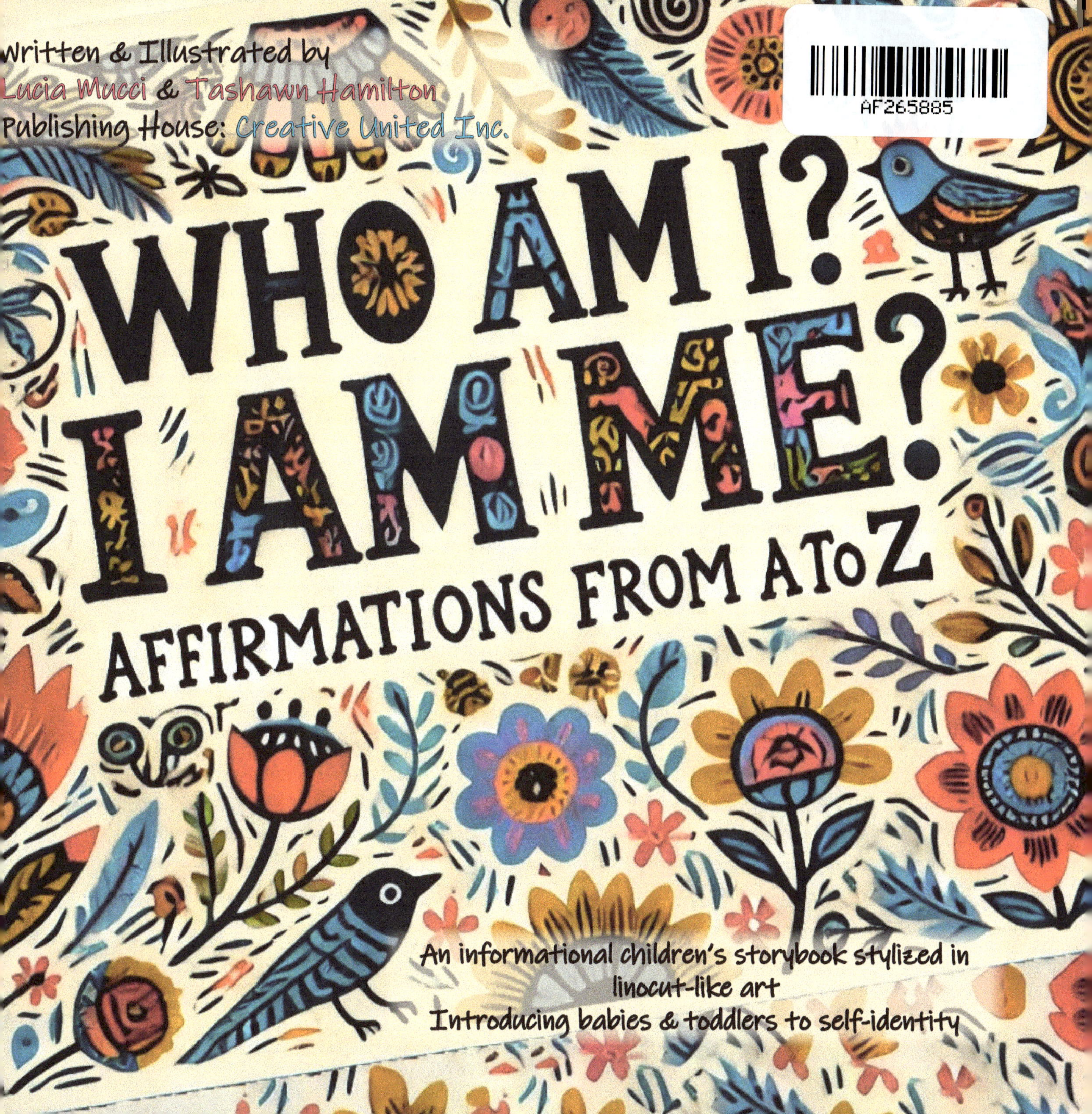
Written & Illustrated by
Lucia Mucci & Tashawn Hamilton
Publishing House: Creative United Inc.

WHO AM I?
I AM ME?
AFFIRMATIONS FROM A to Z

An informational children's storybook stylized in
linocut-like art
Introducing babies & toddlers to self-identity

This book is dedicated to and inspired by
Valentina Hamilton
who arrived October 11th, 2022
From your Mom &
Dad, Happy reading!
We love you
2024

A Learning Adventure Story

A:
"Admired like an anatidae, l'amoureux swan, gliding so slow,
Through the wetlands of Alaska, in a peaceful flow.
So adorable, so graceful, and amazing you are
Just like this swan, you're a shining star!

Animal: Anatidae (the biological family of birds - Ducks, Geese and Swans)
Cultural Representation: Wetlands of Alaska
Flowers: Roses and violets.
Science/Nature: Introduce the idea of wetlands, where swans make their homes.

B:
"Brave as a puppy, strong and so bright,
An American Bully, full of delight!
You shine like the sun, so brave and true,
Inside and out, it's all about you!"

Animal: American Bully puppy
Cultural Representation: A sunny American meadow.
Flowers: Dandelions and tulips.
Science/Nature: Highlight bravery in animals and
introduce the concept of sunny meadows.

C:
"Clever like a cat, with eyes so bright,
Curious in the jungle, day and night.
Exploring new lands with a thoughtful look,
Learning every day, like reading a book!"

Animal: Cat
Cultural Representation: Jungle habitat,
representing tropical regions.
Flowers: Orchids and tulips.
Science/Nature: Introduce the jungle habitat and
the idea of exploration

D:
"Delightful as flowers in the warm sun,
A princess so dazzling, full of fun!
Just like a dragonfly in the breeze,
You bring joy and light with such ease!"

Animal: Dragonfly
Cultural Representation: Fields of wildflowers found in European meadows.
Flowers: Magnolias and roses.
Science/Nature: Introduce the idea of dragonflies in meadows and how they flutter through wildflowers.

E:
"Energetic like an elephant, so big and so tall,
In the African savanna, you hear their call!
Elegant and strong, as you play and run,
Exploring the world, having so much fun!"

Animal: Elephant
Cultural Representation: African savanna.
Flowers: Violets.
Science/Nature: Introduce the idea of elephants roaming
the savanna and how they are strong, yet gentle.

F
F:
"Fearless as a fox, so quick and so bright,
In the forests, it plays with delight.
Friendly and joyful, with a heart so free,
Just like you, full of energy!"
Animal: Fox
Cultural Representation: Forests in regions like Canada.
Flowers: Dandelions and orchids.
Science/Nature: Highlight the concept of foxes as quick
and clever animals, living in diverse forest ecosystems.

G:
"Gentle as a giraffe, with its long neck so high,
In the African plains, it reaches the sky.
Graceful and tall, walking with pride,
Just like you, full of love inside!
Animal: Giraffe
Cultural Representation: African savanna.
Flowers: Tulips and orchids.
Science/Nature: Introduce giraffes, the tallest
animals in the world, and their gentle nature.

H:
"Hopeful as a hedgehog, who rolls up tight,
Happy and warm, full of delight.
In a safe, happy home, you grow with love,
As peaceful as the stars above!"

Animal: Hedgehog
Cultural Representation: European woodlands.
Flowers: Magnolias and roses.
Science/Nature: Introduce hedgehogs and how
they curl up to protect themselves, symbolizing
warmth and safety.

I:
"Imaginative like an iguana, so green and so sly,
In the jungle it climbs, reaching so high.
Incredible you are, full of wonder and glee,
Exploring the world, so wild and free!

Animal: Iguana
Cultural Representation: Tropical jungles in places like South America.
Flowers: Dandelions and tulips.
Science/Nature: Introduce Iguanas as clever climbers that live in jungles, showcasing their ability to explore.

J
Jy
J:
"Joyful as a jaguar, fast and strong,
In the rainforest, where it runs all day long.
Jubilant and full of life, you bring joy to all,
Standing tall and proud, you answer the call!
Animal: Jaguar
Cultural Representation: Rainforests in Central and South America.
Flowers: Orchids and violets.
Science/Nature: Jaguars are powerful creatures that thrive in rainforests; highlight their agility and strength.

K:
"Kind like a kangaroo, hopping so high,
In Australia's outback, under the bright blue sky.
Keen and clever, you leap with glee,
Spreading kindness and love for all to see!

Animal: Kangaroo
Cultural Representation: Australian outback.
Flowers: Roses and tulips.
Science/Nature: Kangaroos are native to Australia,
known for their strong legs and their ability to leap.

L:
"Lovable like a lion, with a heart full of pride,
In the African savanna, where the brave ones reside.
Lively and bold, you lead the way,
Full of love and joy, every single day!"

Animal: Lion
Cultural Representation: African savanna.
Flowers: Magnolias and dandelions.
Science/Nature: Lions are symbols of strength and leadership in the savanna.

M

M:
"Marvelous as a Maltese, gentle and bright,
In the charming streets, under the warm sunlight.
Mellow and playful, with joy in your stride,
Spreading happiness, with love as your guide!"

Animal: Maltese
Cultural Representation: Italian countryside or
a picturesque Italian town square.
Flowers: Lavender and poppies.
Science/Nature: Maltese dogs are known in
Mediterranean regions for their gentle, friendly
temperament and long, silky fur, symbolizing
elegance and charm.

N

N:
"Nurturing like a narwhal, swimming so free,
In the icy waters, in the deep blue sea.
Noble and gentle, with a caring heart,
You love and grow, you're a work of art!"

Animal: Narwhal
Cultural Representation: Arctic waters.
Flowers: Magnolias and roses.
Science/Nature: Narwhals are known as the
"unicorns of the sea" and are found in Arctic waters.

O:
"Optimistic as an owl, wise and true,
In the quiet woods, with a peaceful view.
Open-minded and bright, you soar so high,
with endless possibilities, you reach for the sky!"

Animal: Owl
Cultural Representation: European woodlands.
Flowers: Violets and roses.
Science/Nature: Owls symbolize wisdom and
observation in quiet woodlands.

P:
"Playful as a penguin, waddling with joy,
In the icy seas, like a happy little boy.
Precious and special, with a heart so bright,
You shine like a star, spreading pure delight!"

Animal: Penguin
Cultural Representation: Antarctic regions.
Flowers: Dandelions and tulips.
Science/Nature: Penguins are known for their
playful nature in cold Antarctic waters.

Q
Quirky Quokka.
Q:
"Quick-witted like a quokka, with a smile so wide,
In the forests of Australia, where happiness can't hide.
Quiet moments with you are cherished, so dear,
Full of love and light, you bring endless cheer!"
Animal: Quokka
Cultural Representation: Australian forests.
Flowers: Orchids and violets.
Science/Nature: Quokkas are known for their
smiling faces and friendly demeanor.

R:
"Radiant as a rabbit, full of light,
In the meadows, hopping with all its might.
Resilient and strong, you rise when you fall,
Full of love and hope, you stand so tall!"

Animal: Rabbit
Cultural Representation: European meadows.
Flowers: Roses and tulips.
Science/Nature: Rabbits symbolize energy and
resilience, often found hopping through meadows.

S:
"Shy like a snow leopard, in mountains so steep,
Through the high Asian peaks, where quiet winds sweep.
Playful and curious, with paws soft and light,
You leap and explore, a beautiful sight!"

Animal: Snow Leopard cub
Cultural Representation: Central and South Asian mountains (Russia, Mongolia, Kazakhstan, Uzbekistan, India, Nepal, and Bhutan)
Flowers: Edelweiss and Himalayan poppies
Science/Nature: Snow leopards are elusive and shy, well adapted to mountainous terrains with powerful leaps and a playful nature when young.

T:
"Tenacious as a tiger, fierce and bold,
In the jungles of Asia, with stories untold.
Talented and mighty, with a heart full of might,
You're a treasure so bright, shining day and night!"

Animal: Tiger
Cultural Representation: Asian jungles.
Flowers: Orchids and violets.
Science/Nature: Tigers are apex predators,
symbolizing strength and tenacity, thriving
in the jungles of Asia.

U:
"Unique as a unicorn, one of a kind,
In a magical land, with dreams in your mind.
Unstoppable you are, full of love and glee,
You can be anything, just wait and see!"

Animal: Unicorn (mythical)
Cultural Representation: A fantasy land.
Flowers: Tulips and dandelions.
Science/Nature: While unicorns are mythical, they
symbolize the magic of being unique and full of potential.

V:
"Valiant as a vulture, soaring so high,
In the desert's bright sun, up in the sky.
Vibrant and bold, with courage to spare,
You face every challenge with love and care!"

Animal: Vulture
Cultural Representation: Desert regions, such as the Sahara.
Flowers: Roses and violets.
Science/Nature: Vultures are resilient and powerful creatures,
soaring high above desert landscapes

W

W:
"Wise like a whale, swimming so free,
In the deep, vast ocean, under the sea.
Wonderful and kind, with a gentle heart,
You're a work of art, from the very start!"

Animal: Whale
Cultural Representation: Oceans around the world.
Flowers: Magnolias and tulips.
Science/Nature: Whales are gentle giants of the sea,
symbolizing wisdom and wonder in the oceans.

X
"Extraordinary like a xerus, quick and bright,
In the African desert, under the sunlight.
Excited for the future, so full of dreams,
You'll excel at anything, no matter how it seems!"

Animal: Xerus (a type of African ground squirrel)
Cultural Representation: African deserts.
Flowers: Orchids and dandelions.
Science/Nature: Xerus are small, quick animals,
found in the African deserts, symbolizing energy
and resourcefulness.

Y:
"Young as a yak, full of yearning to grow,
In the mountains of Tibet, where the cool winds blow.
You're eager to learn, full of dreams to chase,
And with each new day, you'll find your own place!"

Animal: Yak
Cultural Representation: Tibetan mountains.
Flowers: Violets and roses.
Science/Nature: Yaks are strong, resilient animals,
thriving in the high altitudes of Tibet.

Z:
"Zealous as a zebra, so bold and so true,
In the African plains, where the sky is blue.
With zest for life, you embrace the day,
Full of dreams and joy, you'll find your own way!"

Animal: Zebra
Cultural Representation: African plains.
Flowers: Dandelions and orchids.
Science/Nature: Zebras are energetic animals found on
the African plains and known for their unique stripes.

Oh what a day! So much to explore,
With letters and animals, we learned even more.
You've grown in your heart, so curious and true,
And each day is special, just like you!

So carry this love as you venture ahead,
With excitement for learning, let it be said:
Every moment you grow, just remember to see,
The joy of being you, so wonderfully free!

THE
END

A Message From The Authors

THANK YOU

Each letter emphasizes an empowering quality—bravery, kindness, joy, or wisdom—using animals and environments from around the world. The added elements of cultural richness, diverse landscapes, and natural science concepts make the affirmations both educational and fun for young readers. The vibrant cheerful illustrations will bring this world to life for toddlers, helping them connect with both the animals and the broader ideas of uniqueness and self-identity